Animal Activities

KEEPING WARM

JANE BURTON

**For a free color catalog describing Gareth Stevens' list
of high-quality children's books call 1 (800) 433-0942**

Editors' Note: The use of a capital letter for an animal's name means that it is a species of animal (for example, a Neon Tetra). The use of a lowercase, or small, letter means that it is a member of a larger group of animals.

Library of Congress Cataloging-in-Publication Data
Burton, Jane.
  Keeping warm / by Jane Burton; photography by Jane Burton and Kim Taylor. --
North American ed.
    p. cm. -- (Animal activities)
    Includes index.
    Summary: Photographs and text depict how fur, feathers, and blubber keep animals
warm in cold weather.
    ISBN 0-8368-0185-7
    1. Body temperature--Regulation--Juvenile literature. 2. Adaptation (Physiology)--
Juvenile literature. 3. Animals--Juvenile literature. [1. Body temperature--Regulation. 2.
Animals.] I. Taylor, Kim, ill. II. Title. III. Series. IV. Series: Burton, Jane. Animal activities.
QP135.B874   1989
599'.01912--dc20   89-11411

This North American edition first published in 1989 by

Gareth Stevens Children's Books
7317 W. Green Tree Road
Milwaukee, Wisconsin 53223, USA

Format copyright © 1989 by Gareth Stevens, Inc. Supplementary text copyright
© 1989 by Gareth Stevens, Inc. Original text copyright © 1989 by Jane Burton.
Photographs copyright © 1989 by Jane Burton and Kim Taylor. First published
in Great Britain in 1989 by Belitha Press Ltd.

Editors, U.S.: Patricia Lantier and Valerie Weber

Printed in the United States of America

1 2 3 4 5 6 7 8 9 95 94 93 92 91 90 89

Animal Activities

KEEPING WARM

JANE BURTON

Gareth Stevens Children's Books
MILWAUKEE

All animals need to be warm before they can move about and eat. They have many ways of warming up and staying warm.

   Some animals, such as tropical fish, live in warm water so they have no trouble keeping warm. Butterfly fish live near coral reefs in tropical seas, where the water never gets cold.

Each kind of fish can tell exactly the right warmth to be in. When the sunny water at the surface gets too hot, Neon Tetras swim near the bottom, where the temperature is right for them.

Mammals make warmth inside their own bodies from the food they eat. That is why they are called "warm-blooded." Mammals that live where it is very cold need extra-thick coats. Long, thick fur keeps the cold of the outside *out* and the warmth of their bodies *in*.

The Arctic Fox grows long, dense, pale fur in winter. When he curls up to sleep, he buries his snout in his bushy tail to keep his nose warm.

The Musk Ox has a long, thick, shaggy, water-proof coat to protect him from the freezing cold and snow.

Birds are also warm-blooded. In the winter, they need extra food to keep them warm during very cold weather.

A Fieldfare has found some apples. He sits gobbling up the juicy fruit. If other birds come, he drives them away. He looks greedy, but if he shares the food, it will soon be gone. Tomorrow he might not find any more and would starve, so he guards the apples for himself.

The Fieldfare looks fat and so does the Song Thrush. They have puffed out their feathers because it is cold. Fluffed-out feathers trap warm air that insulates these birds from the cold by keeping the cold out and the warmth in.

The White Crested Duck has no feathers on its feet to keep them warm. How can it go on walking with cold feet? Only ligaments move a bird's feet. There are no muscles. The muscles working the ligaments are way up in the bird's thighs. They are kept warm by feathers and by the bird's body.

Feet can still hurt when they are too cold. Chester the chick and his brothers stand on one leg — and then on the other — keeping one foot warm at a time, tucked up among their feathers.

Septimus has never been out in the snow before.
He does not like it. His paws are furry on top but
the pads underneath are bare. He holds one paw
up to keep it out of the snow. A cold cat is a
miserable cat. Septimus runs back inside the
house to get warm.

Tiddlywinks is out on a frosty morning. He
jumps up on the hood of a car that has been
warmed by the engine. Tiddlywinks soaks up the
warmth through his toes. The winter sun warms
his fur. A warm cat is a happy cat.

The Saiga Antelope lives on the dry steppes where it is cold in winter. Its nose is large and puffy, with tiny nostrils. When the Saiga breathes in, the cold air is warmed inside its bulbous snout.

The Saiga's nose is big but its ears are small. The Arctic Fox also has small, neat ears. Mammals in very cold places all have little ears. Mammals in very hot places often have big, bare ears to help them keep cool. Arctic mammals live in the cold so they need to keep warm. Their ears are small and covered with thick fur.

Reptiles are "cold-blooded" animals. They cannot make heat in their bodies the way mammals and birds do.

The Red-eared Terrapin's body stays at the same temperature as the surrounding water. It climbs out of the cool pond to warm up in the sun. In the winter, the Adder goes completely torpid, going into a "winter sleep." Its body temperature remains the same as the temperature of the rocks it is hiding under. In the spring, the Adder crawls out slowly to lie in the warmth of the sun.

Spectacled Caimans live in warm water so they are always quite lively. When they climb out and bask in the sunshine, they become *very* lively. The warmer a reptile is, the more active it will be. But it must not get *too* hot. Overheating is as bad for a reptile as chilling.

Like reptiles, insects are cold-blooded. The Tiger Swallowtail Butterfly cannot fly when it is cold. In the morning, it spreads its wings and warms up before takeoff. It sips nectar from flowers to give it energy for flying.

After a chilly night, many mammals like to bask in the early morning sunshine. It not only warms them but also makes them feel good.

Spiny Mice live among rocks in desert places. It is hot there in the daytime but cold at night. The mice huddle together to enjoy the sun as soon as it comes up.

Rock Hyraxes also come out when the sun rises. They perch on a pinnacle, sideways to the sun to catch its warmth. When they and the rocks heat up, the mice and hyraxes disappear into the shade to hide in crevices and caves.

High up in an oak tree, it can be windy, wet, and cold. When the sun shines, a young Gray Squirrel basks, draped on a branch. Warmed up, he will groom himself, licking and scratching his fur into place. Then he will scamper off to nibble buds for breakfast.

The Harbor Seal swims in the cold sea for most of the day. Thick layers of fat on its body, called "blubber," help to keep out the cold. The blubber gives the seal its round, stream-lined shape. After diving for fish, the seal heaves itself out onto the sand. The sun dries its fur and warms its skin.

Long-tailed Titmice are building their nest in a gorse bush. They bring moss and lichens, and bind them together with spider webs. They gather hundreds of small feathers to line their nest. The mother bird will sit on her eggs to warm them until they hatch. The snug nest and feather lining help to keep the eggs warm.

Mallard ducklings also hatch in a nest lined with feathers. The mother duck plucks special fluffy down from her own breast. Down traps the duck's warmth and keeps the ducklings cozy.

Bluey, the bantam hen, has just left her nest. She has taken her newly hatched chicks to find their first food and drink. Now she settles to brood them again. Many more chicks are under her, keeping warm among her feathers. Baby chicks need the hen to keep them warm until they grow their own feathers.

Making her body into a warm, furry nest, Ginny curls herself around her four kittens. The kittens depend on their mother for milk and for keeping clean. They also depend on her for warmth. If Ginny leaves them for a while, they stay warm by clumping together in a heap until she returns.

When the Long-eared Bat sleeps, it becomes almost cold-blooded, even though it is a mammal. Its temperature falls and it gets cold. When it wakes, it must warm itself before it can fly. It warms up by shivering. A bat shivers so fast that it hums.

Moths also shiver to warm themselves for flight. The Garden Tiger Moth climbs up a spike of mint flowers and whirrs its wings. It buzzes so hard that the wings become a blur. Shivering makes an animal's muscles work hard. The hard work generates heat, and the shivering animal warms up. Now the moth can stop shivering and fly away.

Jack got cold from swimming in the sea. He lies on the beach in the sunshine. He is so cold that he is shivering and his teeth chatter. They make a *brrr* sound every time he shivers. Jack is stretched out to let the hot sun shine on as much of his body as possible.

Jack and his sisters are asleep on a cool evening. They have tucked in their paws and are curled up together to keep their warmth in.

Fan and Lady are chasing Jack. There is a biting-cold wind, but the dogs are happy because running hard keeps them warm.

The Steppe Lemming is so tiny that it could easily die of the cold. It survives the winter underneath the snow. Snow is like a blanket or thick fur or fluffed-out feathers. It keeps cold out and warmth in. The lemming feeds in tunnels in the grass underneath the snow blanket. It sleeps in a nest of dry grass. Protected from the freezing weather, it keeps warm all through the long winter.

Fun Facts

1. To keep warm in winter, the squirrel lives in a hole high up in a tree. It sleeps in the hole at night, away from the wind and snow.

2. The fox can sleep in the snow with its nose under its tail. Its fur coat keeps it warm.

3. Some northern birds grow extra feathers for winter. On cold days, they fluff out their feathers and pull in their neck.

4. Some birds cannot find enough food or cannot protect themselves well enough from winter cold. So they *migrate*, or travel, south to warm places like Florida, Mexico, or even South America. They fly north again in spring or summer.

5. In winter, bears go into a cave or den and wait for spring. They sleep during this time.

6. A cottontail rabbit's nest is very warm. It is made from soft grass and lined with the mother rabbit's own fur.

7. In winter, the cottontail rabbit does not live in a nest. It lives under a barn or under some cornstalks on a farm.

8. Many animals, such as woodchucks, moles, and skunks, keep warm in their underground burrows.

9. Beavers build houses or dams on the water. When ice and snow cover the houses in winter, they are nice and cozy inside.

For More Information About Animal Life

These books and magazines will tell you many interesting things about animals. When possible, we have listed videos. Check your local library or bookstore to see if they have these materials or will order them for you.

Books:

Animal Homes. Elswit (Western)
Animals of the Polar Regions. Johnson (Lerner)
Baby Animals. (Macmillan)
The Fox with Cold Feet. Singer (Parents Magazine Press)
Good Morning — Sun's Up. Beach (Scroll)
When Winter Comes. Freedman (Dutton)
Why do Animals Sleep Through the Winter? Arvetes (Macmillan)
Winter Barn. Parnall (Macmillan)

Magazines:

Chickadee
Young Naturalist Foundation
P.O. Box 11314
Des Moines, IA 50340

Owl
Young Naturalist Foundation
P.O. Box 11314
Des Moines, IA 50340

National Geographic World
National Geographic Society
P.O. Box 2330
Washington, DC 20013-9865

Ranger Rick
National Wildlife Federation
8925 Leesburg Pike
Vienna, VA 22184-0001

Videocassette:

Animals in Autumn and Winter. (Encyclopaedia Britannica Educational)

Things to Do

1. If you have a pet, try to observe its ways of keeping warm in various situations. Write your observations down in a short paragraph or two.

2. If you live in a climate that is cold for at least part of the year, make a list of your favorite warm drinks and foods.

3. Do some research in the library or talk with your parents and find out why certain types of clothing keep you warm when the weather is cold.

4. When you are out with your friends on the school playground in cold weather, what are some of the activities you can do to warm up quickly during recess?

5. Having a fire burning in your fireplace at home provides a good source of warmth. What are some other advantages of having a fireplace?

Things to Talk About

1. All animals need to be warm before they can move around and feed. Is this true for humans, too? Why is it so hard to move about when it is cold?

2. All animals know what they must do in order to keep warm. Do you know what to do to keep warm during cold weather? Explain.

3. Many people prefer warm weather to cold. What are some of the advantages of living where the weather is warm? What are some of the disadvantages of a warm or hot climate?

4. Do you think certain types of foods and drinks can help us to stay warm? Which ones? What things do animals eat and drink to keep warm?

5. Some animals, especially birds, migrate — or move — south in winter to stay warm. Do people migrate? Why or why not?

6. If you live in a cold climate, discuss how your pet or someone else's pet keeps warm. How do the animals know what to do?

7. Why is it a good idea to always wear a hat, scarf, and gloves in cold weather? What can happen if all parts of your body are not kept covered and warm?

8. When you first get into bed at night, the sheets and pillows might be cold for a while. Sometimes you may begin to shiver and curl up under the blankets. After a short time, you can feel heat beginning to surround you and the shivering stops. What makes the bed warm up?

9. Some animals like to keep warm by simply sitting out in the sunshine. Is this always a good idea for people? Why or why not?

Glossary of New Words

bask: to rest in a pleasant warmth.

blubber: the thick fat on many sea mammals that protects them from the cold.

brood: to sit on eggs; to hatch eggs; to keep chicks warm and protected.

crevice: a small crack or split.

down: soft, fine, fluffy feathers.

gobble: to eat quickly and greedily.

gorse: thick spiky shrubs.

insulate: to protect with a material that prevents heat, electricity, or sound from passing through.

ligament: a piece of tough tissue that connects bones or holds muscles or organs in place.

mammals: any of a large group of hairy, warm-blooded animals whose babies feed on their mother's milk.

migrate: to travel regularly from one region or climate to another.

nectar: the sweet liquid found in flowers used by bees to make honey.

perch: to rest or sit, usually on something high above the ground.

pinnacle: the highest point.

reptiles: any of a group of cold-blooded animals that have bony skeletons and scaly bodies. Snakes, lizards, and turtles are reptiles.

snout: the protruding nose and jaws of an animal; the muzzle.

steppe: a great plain with few trees.

terrapin: a freshwater or tidewater turtle.

torpid: asleep or inactive.

tropical: very hot and sultry; humid.

Index